Prayers
For
Times like These

What do you do when you do not know what to do:

PRAY!

By
Pamela Duran

Table of Contents

A PRAYER FOR PASSION 8

A PRAYER FOR FOCUS 9

A PRAYER FOR MY IDENTITY 10

A PRAYER FOR MY FAMILY 11

A PRAYER FOR ACTION 12

A PRAYER FOR THE ANOINTING 13

A PRAYER FOR MATURE ACTION 14

A PRAYER FOR JOY UNSPEAKABLE 15

A PRAYER FOR RELEASE OF PAST MISTAKES 16

A PRAYER FOR FAITH OVER FEAR 17

A PRAYER FOR PLEASING GOD 18

A PRAYER FOR PURITY – DEFLECTING TEMPTATION
....19

A PRAYER FOR OVERCOMING PRESSURE 20

A PRAYER FOR HEALING HURTS 21

A PRAYER FOR MENDING RELATIONSHIPS 22

A PRAYER FOR DILIGENT CONSISTENTCY 23

A PRAYER FOR FAVOR 24

A PRAYER FOR WISDOM 25

A PRAYER FOR INNER GROWTH 26

A PRAYER OF GRATITUDE 27

A PRAYER FOR SALVATION 28

Last Days messages by Jackie McClure 1/15/2023 29

HOW TO CONSTRUCT A PRAYER PETITION 31

GIVE YOURSELF GRACE 33

NEVER QUIT ON YOU! 43

ABOUT THE AUTHOR 45

SPECIAL OFFER FOR YOU 48

MOTIVATE AND INSPIRE OTHERS!

"Share This Book"

Retail $4.95

Sepcial Quantity Discounts

501 - 1000 Books	$3.95
1001 - 1500 Books	$2.95
1501 + Books	$1.95

To Place an Order Contact:
pamela.duran@att.net

Dedicated to the memory of:

My dad (Marion L. McClure) and his brothers my Uncle Jackie Milton McClure and Uncle M.J. McClure

These were true men of GOD and men of FAITH! They persevered in the hard times and continued to press on to the PRIZE the mark the HIGH Calling of GOD.

They have run their race and attained their prize. My prayers and hopes are for ALL our families to see them again in heaven and we can all celebrate together in the heavenly chorus and band.

We love you and miss you all every day!

Sincerely,

Your dear sweet daughter and niece, Pamela

What to do when you do not know what to do:

PRAY!

A PRAYER FOR PASSION

I pray in FAITH, ASKING and BELIEVING for my PASSION to be restored.

I thank you Lord for your graciousness and all you want to give me Lord.

I AM an excellent receiver.

Thank you for forgiveness and redemption.

I AM activating my faith to ask to recover and maintain my PASSION.

To regain and sustain my cutting edge!

I believe and pray Psalm 51:10 "Create in me a clean heart O GOD and renew a steadfast spirit within me!

Jeremiah 29:12-13 "Call upon me and come and pray to me and I will listen to you. You will seek me and find me when you search for me with all of your heart."

I say YES LORD YES!

GO WHERE GOD GUIDES

Because that is where GOD PROVIDES!

A PRAYER FOR FOCUS

I pray for terminator FOCUS. Dear Lord, I thank you and I praise you for reigning in power and supplying me with weapons of Victory.

Ephesians 6:10 – 18

Lord arm me with my spiritual weapons to fight for you: My helmet of salvation to protect my mind, my breastplate of righteousness to protect my heart and emotions, my belt of truth to hold myself together, my feet are shod with the preparation of the gospel, my shield of FAITH to protect me from the fiery darts of the evil one, and my sword which is the word of GOD to hide in my heart and use as a guide in my daily walk and prayer and thanksgiving.

Lord, I admit I have been angry and distracted by situations and fighting all the wrong people.

Lord, I ask you for courage, discernment, for diligence and laser like focus YES LORD YES!

I thank you Lord for being with me and fighting the real enemy through me.

YES LORD YES!

A PRAYER FOR MY IDENTITY

Thank you, Lord, for bringing to my remembrance of WHO I AM – 1 Peter 2:9

I am chosen, I am steady Jude 24-25

I am a joint heir with Christ Romans 8:15017

I am created for GOOD Works Ephesians 2:10

I repent of the comparison I sometimes fall into and the imposter syndrome; for being blind to your greatness and impossibilities you outweigh every day.

I am asking in FAITH believing today you will lift the covers of my eyes, so I will see and experience the greatness you have for me. So, I will wear my under armor of TRUTH and be equipped to go out to help others in NEED. Help me to realize GOD is on the move behind me and before me and I will courageously thrive,

No Matter WHO or WHAT is against me!

YES LORD YES!

Romans 8:37 "...We are more than conquerors"

YOU ARE FOR ME!

A PRAYER FOR MY FAMILY

Thank you, Lord, for choosing my children for me. They are the light of my life and I praise you for my grandchildren and all the Blessings you are preparing for them. I praise you for their mothers and what a blessing they have been to their children and for giving them strength and recharging and refueling them to go to battle for their families every day!

I pray for each of my immediate family's salvation Lord! For their blessings and guidance – So Blessed!

I pray for my children, their families, and my spouse to "Commit their works to the Lord and HE will establish their plans." Proverbs 16:3

I pray for their ways to be pleasing to you Lord.

Proverbs 16:7

I pray for them all "not to fear sudden danger or ruin of the wicked when it comes, for the Lord will be your confidence and will keep your foot from a snare." Proverbs 3:25-26

I pray continually for your safety, protection, good health and wealth and salvation first.

I pray Proverbs 3:5-6 over you: "Trust in the Lord with ALL your heart and lean not unto your own understanding. In all your ways acknowledge HIM and He will make your paths straight."

I love my family and have FAITH and asking and believing for my family's salvation. Yes Lord Yes!

11

A PRAYER FOR ACTION

I thank you Lord for your faithfulness and your hope for me.

I will respond positively to you and the plans you have for me.

Holy Spirit help me to set aside discouragement and fear and remember that by God's Grace and in your power Holy Spirit

I will be used by YOU to do the extraordinary.

SO IT IS!

YES LORD YES!

Jeremiah 29:11

"For I know the plans I have for your saith the Lord to give you a hope and a future."

Habakkuk 2:2

"...Write the vision and make it plain... that he may RUN that reads it."

Write it DOWN and MAKE IT HAPPEN!

Proverbs 23:7

"For as a man thinketh in his heart, so is he..."

A PRAYER FOR THE ANOINTING

Thank you, Lord, for empowering me with a greater anointing of the Holy Spirit and for direct access as the power of God's Spirit that lives inside of me!

1 John 2:27 (KJV)

"But the anointing which ye have received of him abideth in you, and ye need not that any man teach you; but as the same anointing teacheth you of all things, and is truth and is no lie, and even as it hath taught you, ye shall abide in him."

John 14:16

"And I will pray the Father and he shall give you another Comforter, that he may abide with you forever!"

John 14:26

"But the Comforter, which is the Holy Ghost, whom the Father will send in my name, he shall teach you all things, and bring all things to your remembrance, whatsoever I have said unto you."

Joel 2:28 "And it shall come to pass afterword, that I will pour out my spirit upon all flesh: and your sons and your daughters shall prophesy, your old men shall dream dreams, your young men shall see visions.

Acts 2:4 "and they were all filled with the Holy Ghost and began to speak with other tongues as the Spirit gave them utterance."

Yes Lord Yes!

A PRAYER FOR MATURE ACTION

Lord, I praise you and Thank you

for allowing me to present myself

as determined commitment to TAKE ACTION

to serve YOU and follow the steps you are
orchestrating before me – to move into Good Works
for you to increase my FAITH,

and

share deliverance, freedom, love, and light without
fear standing confidently in your strength!

If GOD BE FOR US

WHO can be against us!

Yes Lord Yes!

Psalm 119:133

"Order my steps in thy word: and let not any iniquity have
dominion over me."

Proverbs 16:9

"A man's heart devises his way: but the Lord directs his
steps."

Isaiah 54:17

"No weapon formed against you shall prosper..."

Matthew 19:26

"With God All things are possible"

A PRAYER FOR JOY UNSPEAKABLE

Lord, I pray for my JOY to be restored

With JOY UNSPEAKABLE and FULL OF GLORY

FULL OF GLORY!

Matthew 25:23,29 says;

"When you multiply what GOD has given you, that is JOY and you shall receive ABUNDANCE!"

Philippians 4:13

"The JOY of the LORD is my strength."

JOY in the LORD is my STRENGTH!

JOY IN THE LORD!

JOY comes from the Holy Spirit abiding in God's presence and from HOPE in HIS WORD!

HOLY SPIRIT RAIN DOWN the JOY!

J – Jesus

O – Others

Y – Yourself

A PRAYER FOR RELEASE OF PAST MISTAKES

I praise you and look forward to a joyous glorious future oh Lord.

Thank you, Lord for complete forgiveness, cleansing and changing me inside and out.

I repent of any foolishness that perpetuates old sin patterns and by the Holy Spirit's power I release and walk away from the old patterns holding me captive.

I am asking in FAITH, believing for Freedom, and the renewing of my mind and for the release of old past patterns, thoughts, and actions.

For the ability to deflect the lies and embrace TRUTH.

II Corinthians 5:7

"I am a new creature in Christ, old things are passed away behold all new things have come."

Yes LORD Yes

By the resurrection POWER and with the Holy Spirit's anointing.

I can walk a new way of life free from my past mistakes.

YES LORD YES

I AM FREE!

John 8:36

"Whom the SON makes FREE is FREE INDEED!"

A PRAYER FOR FAITH OVER FEAR

Claiming my Calling!

Lord, I praise you and thank you for choosing me before you formed me in my mother's womb and setting me apart and appointing me to make generational changes to leave a legacy for my family.

Jeremiah 1:4-8

"I repent of any fears I have fallen into because you did not give us the spirit of FEAR – but of POWER and LOVE and of a sound mind."

2 Timothy 1:7

"Lord, I ask in FAITH believing **Jeremiah 29:11** – to know the plans you have for me to give me a hope and a future to prosper me and thank you for giving me the right words and wisdom to move forward in your will and way."

YES LORD YES!

Say this PRAYER daily:

"I believe I am always divinely guided.

I believe I will always take the right turn of the road.

I believe God will always make a way where there is no way!"

Norman Vincent Peale

The Power of Positive Thinking

17

A PRAYER FOR PLEASING GOD

Thank you, Lord, for guiding me in your ways that are higher than mine – **Isaiah 55:8**

In HIGHER PRAISE.

Caring and sharing my LOVE for Jesus to the lost, the broken-hearted, family, co-workers, neighbors.

To extend FAITH and TAKE ACTION without

Knowing the how and increase

my Faith to be an excellent receiver.

Testify and share what God is doing with others to help increase their FAITH and Belief!

YES LORD YES!

Isaiah 55:9

"For as the heavens are higher than the earth, so are my ways higher than your ways, and my thoughts than your thoughts."

Isaiah 55:11

"So shall my word be that goeth forth out of my mouth, it shall not return unto me void, but it shall accomplish that which I please, and it shall prosper in the thing whereto I sent it."

Selah!

A PRAYER FOR PURITY – DEFLECTING TEMPTATION

Oh Lord, Thank you for your LOVE and YOUR SPIRIT living inside me Romans 6:12-14.

Thank you for exposing my weakness and temptations and rescuing me from them 2 Peter 2:9

We die daily to you and I pray to walk in the spirit, so I do not carry on desires of the flesh **Galatians 5:16**

I thank you for sin will not be my master – I am covered under grace – Thank you Lord for helping me to walk in a manner worthy of the calling you have called me.

Ephesians 4:1

The Lord is my refuge, the Lord is the strength of my heart.
Psalm 91: 7-9

My portion forever, **Psalm 73:26**

God prays for me that my FAITH may not fail.

Luke 22:31-32

YES LORD YES

I will stand firm – having put on my belt of TRUTH and my BREASTPLATE of righteousness to protect my heart, mind and emotions. Ephesians 6:14

SO IT IS

YES LORD YES

A PRAYER FOR OVERCOMING PRESSURE

Lord Jesus, I submit all the worldly pressures,

I have allowed to consume my time,

my spirit and energy.

I submit the people pleasing, not saying NO to

The activities that do not move the needle for you and your Kingdom.

I submit the pressure to perform feeding the idol of reputation.

I submit the pressure to DO IT ALL feeding the idol of self-reliance.

I submit the pressure to keep up with current times the idol of achievement.

Lord, I release the self-imposed pressures I put on myself EVERY DAY to YOU!

I joyfully receive the freedom you promised us in **John 8:32**, "You will know the truth and the truth will make you free."

I pray **Psalm 37:4** "To delight myself in the Lord and he will give me the desires of my heart."

I claim Godly authority over the insane amount of pressure I have put myself under.

I am free in Jesus Name!

O Lord YOU ARE and SO I AM! And so it is!

A PRAYER FOR HEALING HURTS

A prayer for forgiveness and healing my hurts within.

Dear Lord help me to be quick to forgive my offenders and haters.

7 x 70 according to Luke 17:4 (TPT)

"No matter how many times in one day your brother sins against you and says, 'I'm sorry: I am changing: forgive me,' you need to forgive him each and every time"

It is through your strength and HOLY SPIRIT I can forgive and move on in freedom, love and humility, putting on my heart of compassion, and kindness, gentleness, patience bearing with one another and forgiving each other.

I pray, oh Lord you put a new song in my heart of praise.

I repent and ask for and receive

forgiveness and freedom.

YES LORD YES!

A PRAYER FOR MENDING RELATIONSHIPS

Lord help me identify when the tools of division and disunity are in play.

Help me to realize it is a ploy of the enemy to try and disrupt my work, my life,

my family, my community, and

my country.

O Lord, bring to our remembrance your word:

Galatians 5:26

"Let us NOT become boastful, challenging one another, envying one another. Let us stimulate one another to LOVE and GOOD DEEDS.

As it states in **Hebrews 10:24-25** "Remember the Lord's blessings – LIFE FOREVER."

Let's lookout for us and for the interests of others **Philippians 2:2-4** "take hold of and let the peace of God rule in your hearts" **Colossians 3:15**

Unity and peace go hand in hand let us demonstrate for the world to envision a community of PEACE, LOVE and TRUTH

1 John 3:18: Love in deed and Truth.

SO IT IS!

A PRAYER FOR DILIGENT CONSISTENTCY

Lord I boldly affirm OUT LOUD

YOU ARE HERE and YOU CARE FOR ME

No matter what difficulty may be pressing down on me at this very moment.

The FACT IS YOU ARE

Quietly working on my behalf without any fanfare.

YOU ARE preparing and planning for my GOOD.

I thank you for increasing my diligent consistency and I KNOW YOU OH GOD are

FIGHTING FOR ME!

I yield my life, dreams, and plans to YOU GOD to unleash your ABUNDANCE and PROSPERITY OVER MY LIFE!

SO IT IS!

AMEN!

A PRAYER FOR FAVOR

Lord I am open and receptive to ALL of your abundance and FAVOR to FLOW in my life. So you can Bless me and Bless others through me!

Lord I pray **Romans 12:11** "that I will get on FIRE for GOD – and be fervent in my spirit, serving YOU oh God and serving Others – sharing my story and helping save many people alive.

Keeping my passion burning HOT!"

O Lord thank you for your Favor on my life and for me being in a position to experience God's BEST!

Breakthrough is HERE RIGHT NOW!

John 10:10 (TPT)

"...But I have come to give you everything in abundance more than you expect – LIFE in it's fullest until you OVERFLOW!"

This is my prayer for YOU!

3 John 2 (TPT)

"Beloved friend, I pray that you are prospering in EVERY WAY and that you continually ENJOY good health, just as your soul is prospering."

Selah!

A PRAYER FOR WISDOM

O Lord hear my prayer for wisdom. I pray as Solomon prayed; to give your servant an understanding heart, that I may discern between good and evil as 1 Kings 3:9 says.

In the *Woman After God's Own Heart* bible steps are listed to help improve your quality of life and move you toward discovering God's Plan.

1. **Test yourself**. What do you desire most: long-life and wealth, or wisdom Prov.3:13-14
DESIRE wisdom
2. **Pray for wisdom.**
Provers 2:3 "Cry out for discernment and lift up your voice for understanding."
3. **Seek wisdom.**
Proverbs 2:4-5
4. **Grow in wisdom!**
James 3:17 describes wisdom that is from above:
Pure, peaceable, gentle, willing to yield, full of mercy and good fruits, without partiality, without hypocrisy.

Be no respecter of persons; witness to those as God brings them to you.

Are you dealing with trials or difficult people? We all need God's wisdom to deal with these challenges. We can ask Him with a heart full of Faith and it will be given.
Proverbs 1:23 "Surely I will pour out my spirit on you; I will make my words known to you."

25

A PRAYER FOR INNER GROWTH
Ephesians 3:14-21 (TPT)

O Lord I kneel humbly in awe of YOU the Father of our Lord Jesus, the Messiah, the perfect Father of every father and child in heaven and on earth.

And I PRAY that you would unveil within me the unlimited riches of YOUR glory and favor until supernatural strength floods my innermost being with your divine might and explosive power.

Then by MY CONSTANT FAITH in YOU O LORD, the life of Christ will release deep inside me, and the resting place of HIS love will become the very source and root of my life.

I am empowered to discover what every holy one experiences – the great magnitude of the astonishing love of Christ in all its dimensions pour into my life. How deep is your love OH God and far reaching. How enduring and inclusive it is! Your love is endless beyond measure that transcends our understanding. Your extravagant LOVE pours into my heart, and I am filled to overflowing with the fullness of YOU of GOD!

I will never doubt YOUR mighty power to work in me and accomplish all this. YOU will achieve infinitely more than I am able to dream, and YOU LORD will exceed my wildest imaginations. YOU will out do them all. Hallelujah. YOUR miraculous power OH GOD constantly energizes me. Now I offer up to you God all the glorious praise that rises from every church in every generation throughout all ages and yet to manifest through time and eternity. AMEN!

A PRAYER OF GRATITUDE

Serve with a heart of praise and worship.

Rejoice with a grateful heart.

Where do you want me to go Lord and how High –
Hallelujah!

Thank you, Jesus! Thank you, father, for getting me
into the right flow and to be aligned with my calling,
my skills and knowledge and abilities.

Thank you for aligning my time spent with YOU and
for restoring my energy.

Thank you for the financial increase – we are blessed
to be a blessing.

Thank you for reducing the stress in my life by lifting
the pressures I placed on myself.

I give you PRAISE – Praise God in prayer and
worship!

Praise in bad times, PRAISE HIM through it, PRAISE
HIM continually.

Continuous PRAISE will be in my mouth – sing –
shout and GLORIFY GOD! GLORY, GLORY, GLORY!

He is fighting for ME, and HE has GOT ME!

Lean in and press on to the high calling of GOD!

The year of the maximum is here – spread God's Love
and Word!

Share your story to help save many people alive!

What are you waiting for?

A PRAYER FOR SALVATION

Romans 10:9 (NKJV) says:

"If you confess with your mouth the Lord Jesus and believe in your heart that GOD has raised Him from the dead, you will be saved."

Prayer from *Michael Todd's book "Crazy Faith"*

"Jesus, I believe in YOU. I believe YOU love me so much You came to rescue me from sin, evil, and death by Your death on the cross and to bring me new, abundant life through Your resurrection. I confess my need for a Savior and ask You to become the Lord of my life. I receive the gift of the Holy Spirit. Teach me to trust Your Word and Your guidance, direction, and instructions in my life, and give me **Crazy Faith** to follow every crazy word You say and every crazy way You lead. Amen."

"You just took the first step in **Crazy Faith**! This will impact you forever. Your eternity is secure. Your name is written in the Lamb's Book of Life. But your decision isn't only for eventually – it's for right now. You now have access to God's very presence, His Holy Spirit, who is ready and waiting to guide you into abundant life. In case you were wondering, you just experienced *saving faith*."

Michael Todd – Crazy Faith

Last Days messages by Jackie McClure
1/15/2023

"You know – I know – God has been showing me lots of things and people.

Whenever God reached down and took Elijah up to be with the Lord– he went to be with the Lord and Elisha saw him and received a double portion.

Most important thing I want to leave behind for everyone is – there are so many scriptures.

Eternity is forever, Paul said.

We have a whole lot more hope than Elisha and what the world has to offer and if we live our entire life and we are with God – We have a lot more hope in Christ in this life to make it to eternity.

We have HOPE in Christ because HE is LIFE and I want to go on with the Lord.

He gets us through the storm, HE gets us through all the troubles and problems of LIFE – So that we can rule and reign with Him.

I don't want to live here without the Lord. I want Christ in my life when I leave this world.

There is no doubt in my mind that Christ is in my life.

It's all about suffering in life – the little things we do can help or hurt people's pain and suffering.

I have not had another pain since, and I thank God for that.

I was thinking about mom, lots of time people could ease the pain and suffering.

If everybody did their part this world would be a whole lot better off!

Somebody touched heaven! Oh God Help US.

Anything special comes from the Lord. I am so glad you are here. You are special!

The Lord will ease your pain and suffering.

He never leaves you the Lord is Always there.

I want to see All the people I love over here on the Lord's side.

And when we go to heaven He is still on our side.

I don't want to see no one that I love to miss the Lord's coming.

The Lord is coming and then the judgement is going to take place.

We need God in our life on the other side of this journey.

I thank God for every chance He gives us, and He will be with us on the other side.

I don't understand what it is going to be like on the other side, but I do not want to see my loved ones miss heaven.

My one desire is that ALL of my Family will be saved. I worry about those kids and I worry about those grandkids. I don't want to see nobody miss out with God. I want to bundle you all up and take you with me, knowing what is on the other side."

Bishop Jackie McClure, Veteran and loved by all!

HOW TO CONSTRUCT A PRAYER PETITION
By Jerry Savelle

Construct / Prepare / Pray

Different Types of Prayer

1. Prayer of Thanksgiving and Praise
   a. Be thankful and grateful for what God has done, will do, and is doing in your life.
   b. Praise and thanksgiving.
2. Dedication and Worship
   a. Committing yourself to be willing to do what God wants you to do.
   b. Not my will but thy will be done.
3. Prayer Changes Things – Prayer of Petition (POP)
   a. Only prayed with the known will of GOD.
   b. Research the Word and Construct the prayer.

Three major weapons in the Prayer of Petition:

1. Use the name of JESUS.
2. Use the Word of GOD in PRAYER.
3. Use the Holy Spirit POWER that is inside you.

Apply these in your prayer life to communicate with God. Prayer is communication. Listen and discern what God is impressing into your spirit. LISTEN!

Construct the PETITION to PRAY:

1. Request
   a. Verbal or written request formed.
2. Formal supplication
   a. Paper of solicitation.
3. Address to a supreme being.
   a. Making a request to a superior for FAVOR.

PETITION START:

Example: Petition for Total debts and ask in FAITH believing.

"Father here is why I am petitioning you for this money and I believe I will receive it."

Research the scriptures for your specific need.

Psalm 20:1-5 says, "The Lord fulfilled all your petitions and remembers your offerings."

He never forgets a seed sown.

God will hear and meet your need.

Powerful way to pray,

Present your petition before God!

PRAY and EXPECT GOD TO ANSWER!

Follow this format:

1. What is your need?
2. Research the scripture for supporting promises.
3. Use the 3 major weapons in your Prayer Petition
   a. Jesus, I come before you
   b. In the power of the Holy Spirit within me
   c. Based on your word <say the verse>
4. State the Need and that you are activating your Faith asking and believing YOU WILL RECEIVE IT.
5. End prayer petition
   a. I am standing on your word Lord in the power of the holy spirit within me EXPECTING You to Answer GOD.
6. Thank you, GOD, for MOVING on my behalf.
7. Hallelujah!

GIVE YOURSELF GRACE

Trauma is what you have experienced, and you are allowed to give yourself some GRACE. You made it through and are now rebuilding, restoring, and restarting your life. God's GRACE is sufficient for ALL your needs. One definition of GRACE in the online dictionary is "(in Christian belief) the free and unmerited favor of God, as manifested in the salvation of sinners and the bestowal of blessings." In order to give yourself grace, you must be an Excellent Receiver! BELIEVE YOU DESERVE FAVOR and RECEIVE the FORGIVENESS extended to YOU. YES, YOU! We ALL make mistakes and turn down unexpected paths, and experience detours in life trying to figure out our path. It is the journey we travel to reach our destiny. Remember: What happens TO YOU, happens FOR YOU!

YOU MATTER!

When you give yourself GRACE, you experience FAVOR and Blessings from above. This is a mindset you must embrace and set your FOCUS to RECEIVE the favor and blessings. Expect to lose friends because they have directed, influenced, and taken advantage of you the entire friendship. You will gain new friends, and they may do the same to you. The important point is to FOCUS your mind on your values, goals, and beliefs. DO NOT WAIVER or let someone (especially an outside influence not sought out by you) impact your life in an opposite direction of your values, goals, and beliefs. 2 Corinthians 10:4,5 states: "For the weapons of our warfare are not carnal but mighty through God, to the pulling down of strongholds. Casting down imaginations and every high thing that exalteth itself against the knowledge of God and bringing into captivity every thought to the obedience of Christ."

You must renew your mind daily. Examine yourself and ensure you are still moving toward your goals, you are making progress, and impacting your family first and then the world. Your family needs you and your help. Why are you relying on the world to help your family when you love them like no other, and you are in their corner with their best interest at heart. Create the course and share the knowledge of finances. By helping your family, you are creating stronger generational changes that will have a ripple effect throughout the family for all time.

Your imagination can cause you to believe right is wrong, and wrong is right, and take paths, causing detours in your life and turning you into a discombobulated mess. Now you are stuck with a mess to figure out and turn into your message. Some people cannot get over the hump to turn their mess into a message to help others. If you experienced what happened and survived, you have a story to tell and share with others to make sure they are aware sooner. To ensure your children, grandchildren, or great grandchildren do not travel down the same road or at least know the pitfalls if they happen to find themselves in the same situation. Be vulnerable, be authentic, and share from your heart. Receive the GRACE extended to you and the favor and blessings that go along with it.

We are all created in GOD's image, and if you are a Christian, you have HIS power inside of you to move mountains, heal the sick, help others realize the gifts within themselves. You can HEAL yourself. Lousie Hay has a book titled: "You can heal your life" if you need extra support or somewhere to start. Dr. Joe Dispenza has conferences, seminars, and YouTube videos (to name a few) on how to heal yourself. He calls it rewiring your brain. He healed himself. So, if you are in doubt, check him out.

You are HERE with a reason and purpose, and your assignment is not over until you have fulfilled your purpose. SOMEONE needs you and your message, so do not delay. This work has taken two years to unfold, and I know it is going to help millions of people struggling with emotional disorders, struggling with their child within, and struggling to move on to new and higher heights. Forgetting the old and pressing on to the new is your calling, your mission. Your actual mission from the bible is to be the LIGHT of the world. We are extensions of Jesus' light, as He was here in the flesh and now lives in US and THROUGH US as we shine HIS light for others to see the way to salvation, see the way to the CROSS, and know there is MORE to life than just day to day routines. There is more to life than just working 9 to 5 and more to life than the so-called American Dream – which, honestly, NOW professionals are saying it is not the American Dream to purchase a home and new car and be indebted to the system. Things change, and people change, but the Word of God does not change! You can stand on the Bible and its promises when the world is on fire. God's LOVE will never fail you, and you can count on it.

Trauma has come to us all in some form or fashion, and it is up to YOU to persevere through it ALL and make something out of it to help your families and the world. We need to come together and trust God. He knows what is best for us and will guide us in the direction needed to help us shine forth as gold. To remove the rough edges and help us to evolve into the person God designed us to be. We are knitted in our mother's womb with an intentional purpose. Let's find out the purpose and use terminator FOCUS to reach the goal. God is NOT finished with you yet, or you would not be reading this book.

It Starts Within YOU is a book about a life turned upside down by an imagination out of control because of a feeling. Feelings are real, and your emotional needs and desires are real. But left unchecked, these feelings cause a breach in your spiritual armor, and that will wreak havoc in your life. Everyone wants to be loved and FEEL the LOVE! IT IS REAL, and when someone is missing those feelings in their life and do not even realize it; without the mental checks and balances to remain on your path it is easy to start believing the lies from an external source that make you FEEL a burning inside and joy not felt in a long time. You must examine yourself daily and cast down any of those ungodly thoughts and overcome the enemy of darkness that is trying to steal you away from God, your family, and all the good things in your life. It is okay to say "NO" and think of the mission God has for you.

You made a mistake, you let an external influence into your emotional cocoon and aroused dormant feelings inside your heart. Realize you are not alone. This happens to people due to their insatiable need to be loved, to FEEL loved, and to seek out an emotional connection. When you are hooked on a feeling, whether it is love, drugs, alcohol, or sex, your emotional state transforms, and you are not thinking about how God will transform and renew your mind. You must unhook and give yourself the grace to know that there is favor and blessing on the other side of this emotional delusion. You are a victim of a fraudulent scam being extended to anyone who will give attention to the lie. The lie is the hook, and as the enticing words are daily repeated (to continuously make you FEEL elated, loved, paid attention to, appreciated, it's a secret between you two, so connected like no other) the hook drives deeper and deeper into your emotional state causing you to start believing a lie. This is a dangerous state to reach. Let me caution you to BEWARE!

GRACE comes in when you realize the REAL TRUTH. Let me tell you right now, if you are in doubt of being in an emotional delusion, let me ask you to watch '90 Day Fiancé' or 'CatFish.' Watching these shows will make you feel like your heart was pierced with a flurry of arrows stabbing you deep into your heart chambers. Your face will feel a heat rush through your cheeks, and they literally turn red with embarrassment. You will experience stomach pain as if you were punched as hard as anyone could punch you in the stomach. You will resonate with these shows and realize the TRUTH. YOU WERE SCAMMED, and everything you believed is a lie. Yes, YOU.

A Christian mom, wife, leader, and volunteer believed a lie so you could feel that loving feeling again, and

NOW what do you do?

Give yourself GRACE!

Face the truth and realize you are human.

Give yourself GRACE!

Bow out of the lie and scam gracefully.

Give yourself GRACE!

Pick yourself UP and keep moving forward.

Give yourself GRACE!

Realize the work you must do and DO IT!

Give yourself GRACE!

Get connected with a Christian mentor or coach.

Give yourself GRACE!

Rebuild, Recreate, and start Restoring your life to be better than before.

Give yourself GRACE!

Realize this is going to take time, and do not rush the process.

Give yourself GRACE! With time comes perspective.

Give Yourself GRACE!

Rebuild bigger and better than before – do not expect things to be the same.

Give Yourself GRACE!
Turn your mess into your message. People need to hear your story and are waiting for you to help them through their emotional delusions.

Give Yourself GRACE!
Be patient with yourself and practice self-care during this crucial healing time. FOCUS on your new mission – Restoration to your heart, soul, emotions, body, mind, spirit, and surroundings.

Give Yourself GRACE!
Know you are loved and treasured beyond all measure by our heavenly Father. Forgiveness is yours for the asking and a blessing beyond compare. Course correct, and now! With this new experience, you can help even more people on their journey.

Give Yourself GRACE!
Be vulnerable and authentic with your message to meet people right where they are in their own emotional delusion and turmoil.

BELIEVE, RECEIVE and EXTEND YOUR FAITH by giving yourself GRACE! The grace of the Lord Jesus be with you.

1 John 4:7 Beloved, let us love one another: for love is of God; and everyone that loveth is born of God, and knoweth God.

Acts 4:33 And with great power the apostles were giving their testimony to the resurrection of the Lord Jesus, and great grace was upon them all.

Romans 3:24 and are justified by his grace as a gift, through the redemption that is in Christ Jesus.

Romans 16:20 The God of peace will soon crush Satan under your feet. The grace of our Lord Jesus Christ be with you.

NEVER QUIT ON YOU!

What resonates with your passion? What do you LOVE the most? So much so that it makes you feel like you can fly and soar above the chaos? You may not know exactly what it is, but you have an idea. This is a leading direction of the life you were designed to pursue.

We all take detours, run into obstacles, and face adversity. It is the journey through, over, or rising above that builds our experiences and increases our stick-to-itiveness, to PRESS ON, to continue toward the purpose we are here to fulfill.

There is a line in a movie, "... *what do you do, try all the wrong things until you find the right one?*" There it is, as John C. Maxwell talks about in his book *"Failing Forward."* We all fail forward and do not realize it. Failing is a part of life and learning how to maneuver around the failure to press on creates experiences to share with others; to encourage them to continue. It is going to be alright; we are all human, and never get anything right the first time. We have the opportunity to try a different path if something did not work. At least you know what will not work and can adjust. Whether it is an invention, an idea, a new business, or a network marketing product, you will fail and learn what works best for you. NEVER QUIT!

Along the way, establish relationships, build on them, connect with people to help each other, and grow all along the way. Every situation will be different; you are always responsible for your reaction or response. Think to yourself what this will be like, get your mindset before a meeting, and make sure to achieve your goals. Maintain FOCUS, and do not get derailed, and no matter what other people say or do not say, remember the deep-down gut passion you feel is REAL! So, it does not matter if other people are not supporting you. You can COUNT ON YOU! Never QUIT!

ABOUT THE AUTHOR

Pamela Duran, MBA, is a Podcaster, author, singer songwriter, entrepreneur, community leader, and IT Professional. Hosted North Georgia's Got Talent fundraising for domestic violence non-profits, specializing in lifting others up, and problem solving. Founder of Lift Up Events designed to LIFTUP others and show them the journey is not as lonesome as it seems. Motivating and encouraging others to reach for their dreams, helping them realize a bigger vision for their lives. A member of Terri Savelle Foy's ministry and an RDC partner, a Vision Coach to help other women see a bigger vision for their life. She started a new BLOG and distributed free bibles and encouraging bookmarks to help arm her community with their sword of the spirit during these times of spiritual warfare.

Pamela has a heart and passion to make an impact in this world. She loves the Lord, her family, writing, singing, and songwriting. Started the "Real Heart Talk" PODCAST in 2021 and it is available on Apple ITUNES, and Spotify, google, all the outlets. The podcast focuses on sharing stories of overcoming obstacles of trauma, fraud, scam, abuse and HOW YOU TOOK YOUR POWER BACK and started taking a positive life stance to rebuild your life. Share your story TODAY. Pamela published "10 Life-Changing Habits" in 2022 to help you learn daily habits that will propel you to success faster; a member of the Dragon Slayers Collaboration to create a book to help victims of abuse, trauma and Domestic Violence reaching International Best Seller status on Amazon; she published "Deep Impact" in 2019 a book written for our younger generations to know sooner what she learned later in life, recorded and released a song "Love You Longer" in 2019 to her online community, and recorded an EP Album titled "Live, Hope, Dream". Attended UPW in 2021, Life on Fire Graduate in 2021, and Speaker on Fire member in 2022, a new member of Christian Women In Media Association (CWIMA), and a member of James Malinchak (Featured on ABC's Secret Millionaire) VIP Coaching.

Connect here:

Website: https://liftupevents.com/

FB:

https://www.facebook.com/pamela.mccllureduran

Twitter: https://twitter.com/pamsduran

InstaGram: https://www.instagram.com/pamsduran/

ClubHouse: @pamsduran

Linktr.ee https://linktr.ee/PamelaDuran

"Love the Helpless, Help the Hopeless and Bring JOY to the Brokenhearted"
Pamela Duran

Pray until you pray through and touch heaven and keep praying until heaven touches you!

Change your posture of prayer: pray for all Saints – Spiritual Combat is both an individual and corporate matter.

SPECIAL OFFER FOR YOU

"WITH GOD ALL THINGS ARE POSSIBLE"

"BE AMAZED FILLED WITH OVERWHELMING SUPRISES." JOB 5:9 (TPT)

ACTIVATE YOUR FAITH TODAY!

GRAB YOUR FREE DOWNLOAD

GO TO HTTPS://LINKTR.EE/PAMELADURAN

AND CLICK ON YOUR FREE DOWNLOAD!

John 10:10 (TPT)

"...but I have come to give you everything in abundance. More than you expect – life in it's fullest until you overflow!"

This is my prayer for you!

Made in the USA
Columbia, SC
18 March 2023

13972283R00028